UNLOCKED POETRY:

WITH

PROFESSOR WAYNE A. GILBERT

AND

THE LYRICAL VAGABONDS

ISBN: 978-1-950375-38-7

UNLOCKED POETRY:

WITH

PROFESSOR WAYNE A. GILBERT

AND

THE LYRICAL VAGABONDS

WORD FROM THE EDITOR

Hello and Thank You…for picking up this latest book by the Lyrical Vagabond of Sterling Correctional Facility.

The title is *Unlocked Poetry: with Professor Wayne A. Gilbert and the Lyrical Vagabonds.* This title is only fitting because the book brings to life exactly how our poetry sessions are performed.

When I first met Professor Gilbert I was blown away by his cool, his Scatman Jazz and his mystical aura that beams outward, inward and aroundward. I was immediately comforted by his loving demeanor and his love for poetry. The fellow poets loved him and that helped me settle into the group.

The Lyrical Vagabonds are encouraging, engaging, and welcoming. The beauty of the group is watching new poets and writers get up to read. For many, this will be their first time ever speaking in front of an audience. It's exciting to watch and the content always astounds me. It is awe-inspiring and motivates me to read more, write more and study harder. Not for competition but for personal growth.

I was very impressed with the level of intelligence, awareness, and open-mindedness of the writers. The style, the content and subject matter that are shared takes "prison writing" to a higher echelon. This book includes you the reader into our world of literature, our imaginations and our vision.

Serving as Editor-in-Chief of this project has opened my heart, my mind, and perspective to the power of writing. Putting the book together was a blast! Working with my fellow Vagabonds has been rewarding and an experience I will never forget.

The 'Unlocked Poetry' program has allowed me to unlock the ideas in my head and put them down on paper, constructing them for self-expression, and to utilize our God-given talents and our learned skills. Thank you Sterling Correctional Facility for allowing us this program and the room for us to grow and say how we feel it!

Thank you very much to professor Wayne A. Gilbert. You have taught me so much about poetry, performance and a bit about myself. You are so instrumental in helping shape lives and encourage people to be good human beings. You've inspired inmates to learn to read, write and perform. That is priceless. You've given us your time, energy, love and paid your way out of your own pocket to come to prison for poetry sessions in one of the nation's most violent prisons. You are the true GURU and every time I see you I see a Rock Star. I have so much fun hanging out with you during our sessions and the writers are all in awe of you.

It has been an honor, privilege and learning experience to be a part of this great program.

Professor Wayne A. Gilbert has only one rule for poetry readings and that is "Shut Up and Read!"

~Douglas L. Micco

Contents

To the ones who made this all possible, the Great Suzi Q. Smith and Daniel Manzanares, and the Lighthouse Writers Workshop. Without your allegiance to us group of misfits none of this could have turned into a reality!

Your unwavering dedication to the group of guys that represent this book and the many more voices that wish to be heard only shows we are not forgotten.

Thank you!

~M.G. Sisneros, Sr.

I know a man with magma in his veins and tea in his soul…

I know a man, a holyJazz Shaman well acquainted with death…

I know a man who sees the unseen and gives voice to the unheard…

I know a man whose love would not be denied by the bureaucracy of razorwire…

I know a man without whom none of this would be possible…

> To the greatest Mentor, muse and friend none of us had the audacity to hope for, but got anyways.
>
> Thank you, Professor Wayne A. Gilbert.

Disembodied Poets

Douglas L. Micco

To free from bodily existence
to cosmically flow from word to soul
to body, to you the audience.
Words, words, beautiful words of poetry…
The war on words, World War III.
Disembodied Poets writing,
having written, will write.
Reciting words,
flowing from pencils,
out of fountain pens,
in cafes, coffeehouses,
under canopies of tree lined streets,
boulevards and avenues,
in prisons behind walls, electric kill fences,
bulletproof glass and distance.
Words of love, thoughts, ideas,
hopes and dreams
expressed through writing poems.
Writing what's in their heads,
angry words shouting out in agony,
crying out for redemption, rebellion or revolution
for their self-expression, creative endeavor
revolting against mediocrity.
Words pouring from souls, splashing from tears,
spitting from mouths,
embers ignite from the cauldrons of the gut.
Disembodied Poets reciting fire from their bellies,
thoughts expanding and exploring inner feelings,
venturing into the unknown

following their trail of words
leading them to pages of their books
subliminal to decipher rhetoric spewed
from the furnaces
of authoritarian machines.
These verses to incite you to resist conformity
promote individuality and
forever challenge censorship.
Question the answers…
Disembodied Poets disembogue
a thought streaming consciousness,
atmosphere filled WIFI,
broadcasting poetry LIVE for you today,
celebrating our Poetic license and
our ability to put words on paper.
With Professor Wayne A. Gilbert
inspiring aspiring poets,
traveling hundreds of miles on his own time, for no pay
but to give me a platform to read my poems,
and to hear the words of these poets,
the opportunity to participate and contribute.
This is Unlocked Poetry,
unleashing my inner voice, and unlimited!
Living in this concrete jungle in 51 shades of grey
tiny flowers sprouting color.
Disembodied Poets coming full circle,
into existence, relevance,
scribing what is experienced, in their hearts, their minds.
Poetic justice and the evolution into writers.
Poetry in action, so "Shut Up and Read!"
Write, Recite, Invite,
Unite and copyright these flames of our rights
to say what we feel

think,
dream
and the rights to personal expression…
Now go and write your own poem!

A Poem about a Poem

Manuel G. Sisneros, Sr.

Thoughts brew in the kettle
words steeping in water
as it comes to a boil.

Now, how do I serve it?
Verbally with a fancy mint,
or do I express it and repress it;
saving it for a nice hot day
which I can then serve on ice,
chilled to get the full effect.
As the lemon wedges saturates
to pull out it's deepest sour feelings.

Wait! I'm not in it to leave
a bitter taste in your mouth.
You see I do this to liberate myself.
Concocting the perfect metaphor to express
when I feel heartless. Ala the Tin Man…
better yet; express my longevity,
and how I made it this far.

The perfect brew only comes
when I add real emotions into
the writings for which I create.

How to Build a Campfire

Tim Wakefield

Pile up tiny bits
apply spark to kindle
the circular conversation

Close friends gather round
the radiating lurid embers
in smoke filled eyes

Pass the peace
tongues of flame engulf
the collective consciousness

Strum guitar
play drum too
keep hearts beat

get up and   dance
before your   souls
  melt

finally stand watch
as morning dew
turns to ashhhhhh

This Place

For Wayne A. Gilbert

Nathan Ybanez

Here, in this place
a bird sings
and in a shamble of people
one face looks up.

Here, in this place,
wind sighs
over brown grass
that furiously
punched its path
to the sky.

Here the sun dances
softly through space
and paints a splashing frog
in aching light.

Does the bird
sing for itself?
A song
of its own exuberance?
Or does it sing
for the soul
who stopped
a somnambulant
boot-heeled rhythm
to turn towards
an invisible sun?

Who does the poet speak to?
alone at the desk,
at the podium?
Glories seep from
the colorless ceiling of mind -
they bloom in empty pages,
scorch through clear air,
where they press and dry -
a menagerie of strange flowers
kept for an unknown purpose
in an unknown hour.

The bird, the word, the sun;
for whom do they exist?

Maybe a curious child
opens an old book
in a musty library
and smiles.
Maybe a hardened man
attacks an invisible cage
with the knife of memory
and cries.
Or maybe, at night
a poet chants to himself
a golden song
lain over his fear
inscribed as a talisman
against the future.

In this place,
the lives
of a galaxy of dreamers

are transcribed.
They meld together
in capricious winds
and fall as rain.

California meets Texas, For breakfast

Christopher Shetskie-McAllister

The arousing caress of steam
rising
from vanilla tea
sweetened with cream
and
a white chocolate chip
macadamia nut cookie.

Fancy.

Here's what I'm gonna do…

I'm fixin' to slow-dunk that there cookie
into this here tea;
modest bites now;
soak the crunch;
hardly chew;
lick-up every crumb
smush-skewered off
the tip of my finger;
slurp-sip every drop
till only moisture remains.

And once that's taken care of…

I intend to find out
If she wearin' them panties
Under my favorite shirt

Dear Patti

Douglas L. Micco

I love you, gotta tell you.
The year was 1977 when I first saw you on
your album cover
in the Used Record Store, in the used record bin
in the Punk Rock section for $1.10
I picked up your recording,
it was different, seductive, alluring.
I took you home and played you at 33 ⅓ revolutions
cranking you up to 11 on my volume knob.
Your music, raw, hard, edgy
it's Rock and Roll, Rock and Roll, it's groovy baby!
You took me on a metaphysical trip uptown,
downtown, midtown
digging your sound, filled with passion, desire, fire.
This was something new. Tripping to your beats,
flipping out to the Beats,
getting me high on Mapplethorpe,
Ginsberg, Burroughs, Corso, Ferlinghetti…
ah, Rimbaud...bebopping to beats untamed,
wild, subversive,
cool man, fusion, Acid Jazz in Blue Rooms,
Dub Reggae in the park.

Your message exotic, erotic, romantic.
Poetic verse intertwining and tangling me
in ribbon of 8 Track Tape,
your stanza's igniting a flame in me
setting my soul ablaze.
Gathering my fantasies, pens, pencils,
paper, coffee and rainy days

pretending to be Dylan Thomas sitting in a
bohemia sipping Absinthe liquor
what a sight!
A blabbering idiot attempting to capture you,
emulating you,
worshipping you, to lust you, to be you...
to get inside of you, your mystery.
I was turned on, aroused, enamored at
15 years of age. A kid, yet old enough to
hold my own opinions, convictions
and thoughts...
Your lyrics become strokes of a paintbrush
collages of visions evoke euphoria,
pandemonium, wonder
moving me to write this love letter to you 40 years later.

Offering sacraments to the alter of your epigrams
drunk on your poetry, stoned on your songs,
I devour them in Communion.
On that Sunday in 1979
you did everything but read poetry,
this was a full-on musical assault!
Guitars churning, your voice blasting out of speakers
spitting into the mic a hail of bullets causing a frenzy
inciting a riot of discourse for the Blank Generation!
Distortion,
feedback reverberating a backbeat that is pounding
blowing down the walls and blowing my mind.
Static disturbance shocking the stage,
your sex appeal pouring out in sweat, tears, blood.
I stood in front of you, your pulpit,
in awe of you, to get close to you…
I showered in your brilliance,

immersed in your words.
My poetess, you are the Wordsmith,
the Penslinger, Literary Outlaw.
Dear Patti,
I Love You.

Down Beat

Matthew LaBonte

I've got notes
I cannot always sing them
But they blow in eruptive galaxies
across my soul
I've been dying to live
the way it sounds,
it lilts and tilts askew
inside the bell
twisting the reed and damping the ring

I've got style and beats
that treat the senses
to Sunday afternoon strolls with sweethearts unmet
swinging our sweaty palms
in metered arcs
that vibrate with
that eyeball twisting kind of shudder
stomach up in my throat
my breath's so short, so sweet
I gasp, I sigh, a silken breeze within my chest
it will not leave.

I've got a song of sometimes sour tones
a shock and awe filled palette
missed hues that fly like caterpillars turned fractal
butterflies
wingtip to wingtip without beginnings or end
melodies that scream with bulletproof intent
that shyly hint at what comes next

muted grey memories of resonating purity
that shine like precious silver
buffed 'n polished
vibrating with that flawless trill
that binds them to my perfect will

I've got that orchestral arrangement
that fail at containing
all the gifts God's given
lessons of love learned at my Mother's knee
momentous intimations of grace and beauty
spiraling and intertwining
dancing with passion that leaps
and quickens with life inside me

I've got music in my guts
it's visceral
when I can't find that vibe, I'm miserable
I've been infected with this perfection
that lives at the edge of my perceptual memory
like dawn-clad skies splashed with cascading crescendos
vivid scales of pentatonic glory that shine from eyes
all knowing
I seek their gaze just to bathe
in their harmonic drifts and rhythmic shifts
I've got life conducted in staccato bursts
I've got life conducted in staccato bursts

I've got a life
conducted in staccato bursts
in staccato bursts
in staccato bursts
staccato bursts

a solicitous muttering between my fluttering lips
that begs to begin again
an improvisational encore that builds on bones I know so well
a phrase   a pause   a phrase
a bridge   a phrase   a tag
a pause
another measure livid
in the concert of my being.

At the beach

Emiliano Urioste

I often kick up my feet at the beach, toes in the sand with no plans but to be.

In fine company, I sit to watch the scene on a checkered picnic blanket I brought along with me.

I began to let the cool breeze soothe my worried mind. I close my eyes & breathe deep in the summer shine.

As tip-toeing ripples creep stealthily to shore, I listen to the soft, shy whisper of the waves strolling by.

My little girl is peacefully at play, humming a skip-step tune of contentment and achievement as sand becomes dune and dune becomes castle. She feels proud of her kingdom and jumps with joy.

She smiles wide as sea shells now become toys.

Crumbs from sugar plums and sandwich crust sprinkle the blanket with delight.

A lone seagull soars by on high to survey what possible pickings it might scavenge as snacks to curb its endless appetite.

The gull is careful not to get too close, it knows what the eye is watchful of the friendly family dog even as he takes the time to taste the fresh salty sea air with his sponge of a tongue for he is an avid beach bum.

The dog watches as a paneled beach ball, blown full of oh-so precious breaths of air, travels effortlessly skyward without a single care, for like us it too is at home there.

The little girl grabs her purple pail with its yellow plastic shovel, flips the pail upside-down and starts to drum adding La-La-La's to the tune she once hummed.

Footprints appear and disappear with the passing of the tide. Laughter fills the void left by runaway racing thoughts.

Woes forgotten if only for a moment in time. With release and a sigh comes all too welcome relief.

All is as it should be, this is bliss, and this is happiness. This is heaven, this is peace.

Can You Hear It?

Nathan Ybanez

Can you hear it?
The springy toe-tap saloon door
action at the tail-end of my shoe
goo worn all the way through
as the music cues and I
gritty click-click rumble my
polyurethane bridge across irregular
gaps in an otherwise pristine
(Thank you community service
Weekend warriors!) concrete.
kick-flip grip taped
to feet (finally!) free
after 10,000 fledgling attempted
flying into the unknown
of the snap-crack rhythm
seven-ply overhang (stairs
meant to be eaten in *one* bite)
Swiss bearings growling their might
on Independent trucks
(neither too loose or too tight)
screwed just the right
amount of goldilocks zone.

The gum-rubber grove of soles
scritch-ping-zinging the sweet spot
grinding off the smack-clatter
turn away of friendly asphalt
smooth as jazz, roll-flowing
and I'm push-breathing oceanic

pleasurable the sighing smiling
punctuation of street: Ollie
Nollie Three-Six-Tee!
Hear my invisible applause!
(They call 'em 'tricks'
'cause they *feel* like magic).
Why you just sittin' there
park bench? Why you layin'
so lazy sidewalk?
All you *do* is sunbathe.
Rise up! Drop in!
Fling to the extremities
all your imponderables!
Can't you hear the sprung-
rhythm music-bones of
a city cat-calling us
to sing-song shadow-dance
all over its skeleton?

Summertime: Big Catch

Douglas L. Micco

Evening light, still
creek gently flows,
Gum Drop tree emits
tiny puffs, settling on the water.
Shimmering sparkles dance
beneath the arms of the Cottonwoods.
In the distance big fish leaps,
turning over creating a splash,
quiet, ripples its way to my toes.
Calm, the locusts sing songs.
Uncle opens another beer,
I pull back the ringed tab
of my pop.
Smoke from distant fires make its way,
swirling my senses.
Comforting me like an old blanket.
Excitement rises as I cast my line,
humming an old country tune
About love gone wrong - walked out the door.
Whatever that is?
My bait's hit, I pull.
Reeling in giant whiskers
face as big as mine.
Swallowed my beef jerky,
lost a boot in the mud.
Dragonflies dart and zip,
as I carry my catch from the banks,
laid him on the hood of our old car
next to Chief Pontiac.

The Interrogation

Rick Anderson

When I was a kid in the mid '60s the school bus stopped in our neighborhood in front of a large, white two-story house on an expansive, tree-lined corner lot. On a typical school day nearly a dozen elementary age school girls and boys would congregate there to wait for the bus. The homeowner allowed us to play on the lawn while we waited an, being energetic youth, horseplay was inevitable. My brother Dave and I, both nine, were usually tackling each other and wrestling on the grass. This chilly fall day was no exception.

As we rolled and tumbled that morning we wound up by some shrubbery near the house. Just in front of these shrubs some decorative spotlights had been installed for the upcoming holidays. During a nifty escape move Dave inadvertently rolled onto one of the lights breaking it off its anchor spike. It didn't seem like a big deal to us apparently as we didn't think to inform the homeowner. I guess it just seemed like another seldom-played with toy that was broken. When the bus arrived we jumped on and went to school, the incident soon forgotten.

After arriving at school we went to our respective homerooms. The day went as a typical fourth grade day did in those times with morning lessons, lunch and recess then back to class. During the early afternoon the principal came into the room and politely interrupted the class to confer discretely with my teacher. After a few moments they turned towards the students and looked directly at yours truly. Mrs. Shroeder instructed me to go with the principal which surprised my classmates as much as it did me since I was by no means a troublemaker of great renown. I got up and nervously followed him into the empty hallway which now seemed much larger, darker and more foreboding than I had ever seen it. He steered me away from the classroom, past the offices and towards the mythically sinister Teacher's Lounge! School legend had it that only one student had ever entered the dreaded house of sorcery and horror and returned. Tales were told of torture, of kids driven bat-shit crazy then sent to a secret asylum for children and even of one heinous death by sheer terror! He was never seen again so who could ever really know? I was certain I would never see the fifth grade.

Yet my burning desire to know and confront what lay beyond that opaque glass and oak-paneled door (along with his giant hand pushing me firmly) propelled me into the room. I could just make out Dave, mirroring my apprehension, ok terror, seated at a table surrounded by scowling male teachers in their most intimidating tough-guy poses. All were enveloped by dense clouds of noxious, toxic cigarette smoke. I steeled myself for the worst as they sat me in a chair directly from Dave and began peppering us with questions, rapid-fire from every direction at once. “Who was involved in this shenanigan? Who broke the light? Who?!?!” They wanted to know if we understood the vile consequences we would face if we didn’t confess or tattle. Our mutual silence stymied them momentarily but they angrily pressed forward. “How did it break?! Why didn’t you tell a teacher or or the secretary or the bus driver or Jim Bob’s grandma or anyone?! What color was it?! (Really - what color?) Neither of us would admit to the deed nor snitch on each other. As a result, their aggravation magnified and, after at least a pack of smokes each, they decided to use some ‘enhanced’ techniques to break us. Separating us, several treacherous looking teacher/goons dragged Dave off down one long, dim hallways while the principal and his little band of henchman led me into a cavernous darkness of another. I soon found myself sitting on a rickety folding chair in a small janitorial closet beneath a freely-hanging, low-wattage bulb dangling from the absurdly high ceiling by a twisted pair of frayed and decrepit electrical wires. Swinging gently (as I’m sure it did naturally throughout the day) the dirty bulb sent flickering shadows dancing along the walls of the tiny, dingy room. The scene was reminiscent of the sets in the old B&W detective movies I'd watch with my Grandpa. I wondered if Elliot Ness or Melvin Purvis, G-Man might appear!

After ensuring I was seated appropriately to receive the full effect of the room's eerie, pants-pissing lighting effects, the amateur gumshoes all lit up fresh Camels and Lucky Strikes then puffed away furiously for several minutes of strategically menacing silence, obviously to build up visual effects. When my eyes were tearing like running faucets and I could no longer hold in a rasping cough the bullied onslaught began in earnest! "We know you boys broke that light! Which one of you little delinquents did it?! We are going to find out one way or another so tell us now!!!" They asked those same questions a hundred different ways and I offered them a hundred shades of insolent silence. They tried deception first by telling me my brother had 'implicated' me and I should 'just come clean'. I knew better though and hadn't done it so that was just another waste of their time and phlegmy breath. They told me I would be punished if I didn't rat Dave out. Umm, nope. They resorted to more elaborate threats, "If you don't tell us what we want to know we're going to..." this and that and so forth. "Detention! Suspension! Expulsion!" Even the dreaded "Paddle!" but they still got nothing and I didn't even know about the Constitution or lawyers yet!

Exasperated and thoroughly infuriated they decided to unleash The Kraken! The ugliest, meanest-looking of the bunch retrieved a three-foot length old, cracked garden hose from a shelf high in the shadows (as high as the vertically challenged fellow could anyway). He held it in one meaty hand with a white-knuckle grip while noisily slapping it into the palm of his other hand, all while impaling me with a fearsome squint I suspected was intended to induce waves of intense fear in me. But his short, rotund stature, big round head and scrunched up, brightly flushed face reminded me of a cartoon character and, unbelievably, this nine-year old miniature hooligan fell into a fit of giggling! They all stepped back in stunned pause (admiration more likely) and it dawned on me this really was like a cartoon or an old movie. These goofballs couldn't do any of the terrible things they were threatening me with. My fear and anxiety melted away. Even then they kept trying, though with less swagger and enthusiasm, to convince me their devilish torture device and sheer intimidation should compel me to cave and tell on someone, anyone, everyone. Finally they were given reprieve when one of the other special trolls of the Northeast Elementary Gestapo slipped into our smoky den of discipline to huddle secret-like with Principal Sherlock. He turned to me, "Your brother confessed. Go back to class."

I managed to suppress a second fit of giggling somehow. I quickly exited the closest and headed back to the classroom. On the way I passed the other group leading Dave back to the office. He was so small flanked by his tormentors. His slumped shoulders, bowed head and tear-streaked face hurt me deeply. These sadistic bastards played out their own sick fantasies by traumatizing a young boy over such a small mistake involving some material thing worth next to nothing! They could have cared less what would happen to us when we got home that evening. Perhaps they did know the great pride and pleasure my stepfather took in addressing the wrongs of little kids and wives. He had planted the seeds of my hatred for authority and these grown-up thugs fertilized those seeds exquisitely. I would never trust or respect an authority figure for the remainder of my life.

Mom was waiting for us at the bus stop when we arrived home that afternoon. She marches us up to the front door of the house on the corner without a word. When an elderly woman answered the door we could feel the heat of Mom's stern gaze telling us to make amends for our destructive deed. The lady's soft expression and graceful demeanor led me to believe she knew what we were in for and she may have felt a little sorry for us but the lesson had to be learned. Mom reiterated our apologies and expressed her embarrassment over our actions and lack of integrity. “They know better.” Then she pulled some cash from her grocery envelope to pay for the light we’d broken. That was the easy part. We began the long walk to our house further down the block.

We basically hid out in our bedroom until Mom called us to dinner. We sat anxiously through a tense and unusually quiet meal then cleared the table. There’d been no dessert, an ominous sign. We usually did a barely adequate job on the dishes as quickly as we could to get back to our play but this night we thoroughly washed, rinsed and dried every place setting, pan and utensil and rewashed at least half of them just to be sure. We did everything possible to prolong the inevitable. Back hiding in our room the call finally came. “Boys, get in here!” One last castigation was due, payable in flesh (ass-flesh to be specific). We bravely (trembling and eyes filling with tears) strode defiantly (heads bowed, shuffling, already covering our rears with our hands) into his room to face the evenings final degradations and humiliations. Let us just say the meeting between butt cheeks and leather resulted in much discomfort and remorse over the next few days.

Now you’re likely thinking I made this up but I didn’t. It’s almost entirely and completely true. And you’re probably saying to yourselves, “I bet they stopped monkeying around at the bus stop after that!" Yeah, sure we did…

On the Road [1]

Tim Wakefield

On the road in my rack
An amazing encounter with Kerouac
Vicariously turning page after page
Bohemian longings within me rage
Capturing the beatnik travels
With every chapter my destiny he unravels

Zig-zagging thy tiny America and never finding it
Ohh thy eternal elusive mysterious IT
Who can ever discover that which is never enough
Discontent in the east of my youth
Caught up halfway across MY America before
The west of my future
Carefreely couch surfing Paper cities
To the next
Frisco the destine nation of my Pennsylvania dreams
Pockets empty stomach too
Delirious hunger for something new
California dreaming of Atlantic amenities

Thumb stretched toward the double
Yellow of the rising sun

On the Holiday Road once again…

Writing with My Ears

Tim Wakefield

A hallowed man leaves his eyes at home
I'm riding waves supreme
flooding into a New York, New York
State of mind.
New York, New York City Night crawlers
dancin' in the high-hat rain.

Creepy like pizza without sax
hustle bustle Ba Buh Buh Busy
Grand piano Fingers Everywhere
This is what a big city sounds like bub
and serious too!
get used to it
The sax has always somethin' to say.

The drums'll tell ya
watch ya step
could be ya stop
Somewheres between Buddump Buddump
Buddumpa doom Coltrane & Harlem.
Time's runnin' out
A busy man's soles keep time
tapatee tapatee
Concrete mixed with asphalt
shhppa tsss suppa tsss

They's somethin' religious about NY in the rain
Thunda Roaws unda ya feet kid
Na Na Na Na Naa that's triumph toots

perseverance babes - progress doll
Don't ya eva go fagettin it neitha
I'm tied of dis shit
3am Path Train to Jersey Tied
        lay lay down
        way way down

Vigil

Christopher Shetskie-McAllister

I imagine you…

Whoever you are.

I wait for you…

Whomever you have become.

I sing for you…

And for me;

Melodies

Like trees

That fall

In the woods.

Us

Christopher Shetskie-McAllister

Perpetual persons engine
exuding identities like bubbles
in a slice of grilling cheese;
each one - The One.

Involuntary observations
-*POP*-
from the newly formed face.
Perpetuating Sage Wisdom, yet
from ignorance. All mistakes.

This cocksure insistence confounds me
in a most compelling way.
You change - I change.
You change = me.

Struggle, my self-deluded mimic,
coalesced into human shape.
All belligerent & presumptuous;
a bit more, than less ape.

Oh so lonely and alone
in that crowded empty space;
you need someone to hold on to:
to mold that wished-for you.

Incomplete, I seek you out,
unsure of whom I'll meet,
but these Ideals aren't real silly.

They're all just cameos
in our bus station heads.

Stirfish

Christopher Sheteskie-McAllister

are there any among you
with a broken soul?
perhaps it was cracked
while you were still small?

or maybe
it was shattered to pieces
in one precise blow?

I've known more than a few
whose came with a hole.
no amount of love or compassion,
soothes them for long;
it just drains all away,
refilled by a void
where spirits, too long
dissolve and die.

how does one shake
an unquenchable thirst?

most heal themselves
when they learn to accept
what cannot be changed.
making love and forgiveness
ends in themselves.

(PART A)

those who remain
the hateful few
who ally with misfortune;
their co-dependent consort
to repopulate the world
with others like them.

they've gouged out a pit
fist deep in their heart
then tossed in their pain
and loneliness
like sticks.

sparked with resentment
a pyrrhic fire erupts:
immolating any good thing
that crosses their path.

then force-feed their spirit
the bitter ash that remains.

should such a creature
it's hungry eyes

upon you
don't let it get too close:
any joy or success
fans the wrathful inferno
pulsing in their chest.

for what loathing burns hotter
than what for the self?

an oily-sick flame
fueled by guilt;
stoked by shame.

(PART B)

My Day Off

Grant Stewart

Stop!
Weekly tick-tocking
mocking motions paused
purple curtains
split horizontally
leading awakening consciousness
from starless depths while
whitewashed concrete greets flesh
roiling frantically away from chilling hardness
fall-step down to stainless steel
plain paste plain bristles
jostles plaque loose,
feel textures
glimpsing pink loosed muscle
over enamel reflections
cheap plastic revealing vanities better left on hold…
vagaries better left untold…
Hold
vice-gripped remains
forgotten freedoms held dearly
desiccated moanings
flashbacks in flash pans illuminating reminiscence
evanesced
old steps follow new paths down insanity's valleys
shadow discoursing liturgies
squandered life laughing hideously behind shrouded
linen
rasping
reaching

grasping straws peeking out sleeves
worn with wondering wanderings
winding down endless spirals and loops
encircling daily circumlocutions around boring listless lives
last viewing silver squares chase away and up gravel-painted rungs…
Brown fabric rustling
uneasy discomfort
coaxing exhaustive oppression
gratefully slinking
slipping
sinking
darkness enveloping until…

purple curtains split once more.

Faces in the Concrete

Grant Stewart

Three planes intersect
leaving edges
stared at long enough to lose dimension
Prana swirls intensely
growing, building, waiting
for just the right moment
to seep in under the skin - invigorating!

Vamachara swings wide down roads less traveled
less due to mass momentum plowing 8-lane highways
fast lane interstates and disinteresting blurs,
blood drives pumping, coagulating, caligulating
consaguating on til congesting…

Must escape down a different track, escape the
machine, a leak from transmission lines
dripping down til flashing up in phoenix-like glory!

As flash fades left back in the room
gongs chime in time to fans-frantic swivel
lights fight back the cleft of gloom
and so is the tune and finish of this missal.

Coffee House Kids

Matthew LaBonte

I grew up a coffee house kid
avoiding vagrancy
3 quarters and a dime at a time.
I drank my way around the world
by cup and carafe
visiting far-fling exotic locales
with my palette
that I would never reach
by plane, train, automobile,
or stubborn little mule.
I saw Kenya and Columbia
through Aribacas and Robustas
and the Indonesian Isle of Java -
a locale synonymous with coffee.
I sank my toes
into cultivated earthen ramparts
climbing steep tiered hillsides
of Peruvian farms.
I sifted through my fingers
then ground the same beans
that are bartered for
in tented French-Moroccan markets.
I indulged strangely spiced craft blends
that were more dessert than drink.
This is where I began to learn
the power of words and imagination,
as I read the labeled varieties
of 30 something hermetically sealed glass jars;
*Maricaibo
*French Roast

*Sumerian
*Kaffe Mit Schlag
*Royal Kona
- and combined them
with their flavors,
in imaginative alchemy of recreation
of discovering these places.
I reinstilled sip by heady sip
the sunshine, loamy soil and lovely Aqua Pura
from which they came
into each and every grain
of all those thousands upon thousands
of wrinkled little dreamy beans.

I learned to cherish coffee
from my Mother.
She had an other percolator,
half-black with decades of firescorch,
dented and used,
stovetop to firepit,
kitchen to campfire,
beloved relic,
bearer of early morning
eye-opening ahh,
and evening after-dinner4 aperitif.
I remember one time
she got sick.
Kidney-bound to a hospital bed,
and the Dr. on Intake interview
naively asked her,
"How much water are you drinking every day?"
Her reply:
"Three

half-black with decades of fire scorch,
dented and used,
stovetop to fire pit,
kitchen to campfire,
beloved relic,
bearer of early morning
eye-opening ahhh,
and evening after-dinner4 aperitif
pots worth of water…"

The movement for me
to the coffeehouse,
was a natural sort of evolution,
a peaceful, teenage rebellion
taking the brew heritage
of my Mother,
and making it my own.
I found a group of friends
of charming confusing diversity
a mix of Punk Rockers and nerds,
beatnik artists and drunken fools,
electro-rave freaks and computer geeks.
We'd sit on the sidewalk patio
bumming cigarettes, trading banter
and pooling money for pots of coffee.
On any given day you'd get anything
from acoustic guitar jams
to stories of violent punk shows,
French poetry to techie-game speak.
And I, right in the middle of it all
in all of my chameleonoid splendor,
one of these,
yet a bit of all, leaning back in one of the coveted

mismatched wrought iron chairs
beaming in with pleasure
at the heat radiating
through the red brick wall
between me
and the copper and brass oven inside,
stoked to toast
the tumbling drum of beans within.
The smell was unbelievable!
The flue vented through the roof
almost directly above me.
I would look up
as the delicate dark husks
singed from the beanstalk
would float from the sky
like the fallen souls of snowflakes.
Gazing up in child-like wonderment
my eyes are speared
by the lazy morning sun
skimming off the giant plate glass windows
wrapping around the north and east
sides of the building.
I squinted my eyes,
opened my mouth,
fat tongue flopping out
to catch this essence
of dark roast divinity,
leaning to meet its slow descent
as it settled onto my eager tongue.
It dissolved,
a smoky ashen ember,
not quite what I imagined.
I leaned forward, picked up my coffee

and poured the last few sips into my mouth,
swishing it cheek to cheek
as I wash the ash away.
I stood up
dropping a handful of change onto the tabletop,
leaving a contribution towards the next pot
and waved a fond farewell
towards distant horizons
as I hustled down the street
hands in my pockets,
belly full of coffee
head full of dreams.

Freedom

Emiliano Urioste

Freedom, what is freedom?
I can't tell you what to feel or even
how to think.
I can only put to pen what Freedom is to me.

Well, to be it, you must see it.
To see it you must believe it.
To believe it is to achieve it!

To be free we need not hold on
o any sense of anger or guilt
for guilt belongs to those caught up in their fears.

Even though a blinded jury,
stacked with so called "peers"
could sew you a life line,
behind the hem lines of an untellable
journeys quilt.

Guilty, guilty, innocent, guilty,
It only takes one to set you free
from "guilt," to break the weighted chain
tipping the unjust scale.

I write to be free, I write to free my mind.
Freedom belongs to me,
Freedom will be mine.

Jenny Lee
(Jenny's Message)

Douglas L. Micco

I'm from nowhere
I'm from everywhere.
Riding on a beam of light
traveling at the speed of sound.
Never knowing where I'm bound,
I rise like the moon
and I'm the setting of the sun.
Drifting about from shore to shore,
telling time by each footprint that I make.
Cruising a rail, moving on down the tracks
no day for regrets and I never look back.
I'm a leaf floating free
catching a lift on the breeze
purple mornings caress my cheeks.
I glow upon the rocks casting pink shadows,
my silhouette sparkles in pyrite
as stardust swirls around me.
Spectral clouds dance in the sky,
my visions are heightened
and my senses awakened.
I look out over the range
wind blowing through my hair
my course remains uncharted.
Astral entities propel me
drawing me upward, outward,
and projecting me like a shooting star
sailing to a new horizon

tumbling into the unknown.
An impulse on a wire
my wings take flight, my soul's on fire.
I'm a mountain stream
singing in the trees
harmonic energies kissing the night
taking my breath away
flowing gently from air to spirit.
I walk in beat
yet out of step, out of line
I'm out of sight
and I'm out of mind.
I'm an old river
winding my way around the bend
slowly rolling home
in time.

Whirlwind Girl

Douglas L. Micco

Descending on a whirlwind
stopping on a dime.
A sparkling crystal to my eye
a shining window to my world,
you are an unopened door,
a natural spring untapped.
You are the river that pours
through the cusp of stars.
You are my high-tide
that caresses me wave after wave
warming me with your fiery bursts,
engulfing me in you cesspool
you are the thermal magma
that flows through my veins.
Exploding into your liquid scream
molten dreams come to life.
You roll on like thunder across the plains
throwing bolts of lightning I hear you roar.
Free energy excites forces
bounding through space
tempest storm
catching currents
leaping to the sky
past mountains
over the celestial sphere
you keep on moving
on your ethereal journey.

Soaring Woman

Douglas L. Micco

You rise from the seas
guiding the four directions
galloping across the stars,
bringing the winds.
You're the earth, you're the sky
You're the water, you're the fire.
A vision of burning desire
You're a wild horse with your golden mane
kicking up dust in a hurricane,
ascending to the clouds
over the terrain
soaring through the cosmos
gathering prisms,
blowing your gentle breeze
through the valleys below,
holding rainbows in your constellations.
Particles of sunlight dance and abound,
a sprinkling meteor shower
splashing color in sound
you circle on,
spreading your wings taking flight,
Soaring woman
into the night.

Dear Jenny

Douglas L. Micco

I wrote you amorous letters,
poems for centuries.
Tilling a thought, entertaining fluorescence
nourishing blossoms, nurturing hope.
Reaching from my grave
grasping at rays of harmony
My smoke signals turn to thunderheads
as they blow west to you
raining down messages
like teardrops in a drought.
My heart beats out ancient rhythms
that call out your name.
My soul catches fire
and the wings of my melody
lift me to the stars.
Riding on a wave
like a cowgirl on a comet
blazing a new trail
that leads me to your well.
I dip into your waters
to quench my thirst.
I fill my pipe with prayers
dreaming these old songs,
sending echoes across canyon walls
resonating to the ocean floor.
Vibrations pound incessantly
as your fountain flows
and ignites the jeweled night sky.

Lament of a Father

Felicion Charles

How am I feeling?
I'm feeling like my life sucks!
Locked away in a place where I get no love
no hugs, no trust,
no bubble-bath back rubs.
Just memories of a past
I feel I'll never be able to pass up.
Oh, and I have a son, WOW!
My boy makes me so proud.
Walking on his own,
he needs no help from momma now,
but the doctors say "he's autistic."
Just because he ain't listening,
weeks later,
they discover something's wrong with his hearing.
You gotta be kidding, they can't be serious!
What is this feeling,
why are my eyes tearing?
Give me something,
I think I need a spiritual healing.
Lord, tell me what they want?
Tell me what they really want from me?
Guess this makes me a dad,
something I never had.
I tell you this not to be sad, just so you know where I'm at.
My life didn't come with a map
when I fell into prison I landed on Rap.
Lost my light but I got it right back.
Broke my girl's heart, still trying to mend that.

No use pointing fingers when there are three pointing back at me.
As I try to get ahead,
like Usain Bolt at a track meet
Maybe that's why they never ask me how I'm feeling?

Proven Dedication

Manuel G. Sisneros, Sr.

From the scribbled scratches on a notebook pad
to my first cursive words in an "I Love You" letter.
The words I write have meaning, truth and admiration.
It all started like this:
the judges announced 24 years in prison!
It vibrates through my very soul.
How much will I miss does it even matter?
Then their faces flash before my eyes:
Michelle, Dometria, Ariel, Isiah, Eian and Gabe...
I failed.
I'm sorry. Oh how I'm so sorry.

I'm brought to reality when
I'm grabbed by the handcuffs,
with one last glance back to see the hurt I've caused.
The corridor seems never ending…
The rattling from the chains around my ankles,
is one of the sickest sounds I will ever remember.
SLAM!
as the metal holding tank door violently shuts.

I've never been so lonely in my life.
Does the camera in the corner even see me?
Because right now I feel like nothing
In my thoughts I've lost everything,
I'm worth nothing but the one thing that doesn't
fade...the images of their faces.

How will I make this possible?
My only means is a pencil, paper, and a stamp.

What better reason than to learn right now?
Practice makes perfect. Perfect we know
I'm not.
So with each and every chicken scratch I try.

"Hi, Hello, How are you doing?"
With each letter it becomes more legible.
With my new friend the dictionary, and his buddy
Thesaurus.

Mail Call! Sisneros #97704
"WOW!" It worked!
They love me, they still believe in me,
Now I can believe in myself.

I've got no artistic abilities, but I can trace my hand.
"This is where Daddy touched the page."
My form of a rubber stamp,
and it proves that no matter how far away I am,
no time or distance
can ever keep me
from reaching out my hand.

Our First Kiss

Manuel G. Sisneros Sr.

I :-) There I stand,
eyes meet

L :-) Heart stops,
O how can one be so lucky?
V :-) One step closer,
E butterflies.

:-) Is this possible?

Y :-) How can I be so enamored?
O Hand in hand,
U face to face

:-) the time has come

M :-) How can I be so in love?
Y With my eyes closed
our lips meet.

Q :-) Not a worry exists,
U yes, I am fortunate.
E :-) Time stands still,
E tightly embraced,
N :-) warm, soft, comfortable…
I belong here.
! :-) Connected, deserving, fulfilled.

Thank you Lord, I feel so blessed.

Shadows in the Moonlight

Vern Mitchell

The sun has set and the evening is upon us.
By the moonlight our shadows were cast
and the soft sounds after dark
made me want to hold you close,
and foxtrot across the world.
Before the night is over,
we would Marimba in Mexico,
Samba in Brazil, and Tango in Tibet.
Holding you even closer we waltz
our way through Europe and we boogied in Berlin.
I've held you close throughout the world.
As the sun rises we'll Two-Step our way home.
For we have left our mark on the Earth!
And our shadows will forever be seen
dancing in the moonlight.

TWO-STEPPING

Movin' and groovin', two-steppin' to the music.
Coming out of a spin
I was dancing with a memory.
Wow, what a memory, memories remembered.
"Play it again Sam!"

Nuthouse Love

Vern Mitchell

I slipped through the morning
and skipped through noon,
jumped through evening
and landed on the moon.
I slid down a moonbeam to the top of a hill,
I rolled through the meadows full of daffodils.
I swam across the river, and hopped a little creek
I ran by your house to take a little peek.
Love can be silly and crazy too.
So put me in the Nuthouse
cause I'm mad about you!

A Winter View

Rick Anderson

One after another the wind
blows the rolling sagebrush
into the kill fence
They tangle in the meshing
and catch in the razor wire
much as recollections in
the web works of my mind
A light dusting of snow
covers the sandy ground
but not the dead grasses
whose pale silhouettes rise
like gravestones through
a shroud of white crystal

On the other side of the fence
people are just waking up
to a day of celebration,
of holiday festivities
and family enjoyment
It's Christmas-time there
in the real world where
people move about, seeing,
touching, feeling alive!

Occasionally, if I'm lucky,
I can remember having
a place in that world
I believe it happened
It seems like reality
Perhaps it's even truth

But a man's mind can be
an engine of trickery
making dreams seem
as a real memory
and I've begun to worry
for when I'll no longer be
able to tell them apart.

A Flower in the Burn Scar

Rick Anderson & Matthew LaBonte

I see you peeking timidly
from between the skeletal bars
of your bleached bony fortress,
vibrant colors a sign of defiance
in this scorched grayscape.
I hear your silent exclamation
of resurgence and rebirth.

Your seed burrowed deep
as the buck sheltered you
from the raging furnace above.
He must have been fearless
offering himself as sanctuary
to your unborn, fragile beauty
in the face of nature's fury.

He nourishes you still, I think.
His essence feeds your tiny roots
as his spirit rises in your petals
and radiates from your golden eye.
His iron will lives within you,
reflecting in your bright bloom
reaching up towards the sun.

I wonder what you see
from your apocalyptic high ground,
up among the blackened stumps,
baked cinders and ash.
The charred hillside gives nothing
but perhaps you look towards

what will follow as you grow.

This barren charnel floor
will be healed someday.
The Mother will make it so.
She bestows her healing powers
as part of a grand design
that always lives on.
You are the hope she sends.

Buried Alive

Rick Anderson & Nathan Ybanez

My contemplative moments
are like motes of dust
swirling in bright beams
burning through the shadows.
Each a thing I mean to do:
a regret, an unfilled dream,
a tear, a kiss, a goodbye.
I live in these siren flashes
sucking at them like a leech
growing fat on the suffering.

Time is a terrible circle
closing in on itself,
cutting away at an empty heart.
I search in vain for the moment
I grew too large in my loss
I turned to this flailing morbidity
from an illusive future
to a ransacked past.

There's no light here - not really.
These nostalgic pyres
are as meaningless
as tears in the rain.
But things continue to grow
and I claw for my salvation.

Across my Rubicon,
alone in my grave,
beholding my only echoes of all

the people I used to be,
I wonder what god
would deem it just
for an old man
to suffer the follies
of an arrogant youth.

damned

Michael Severson

never quite satisfied
with what he had.

that was the immature
guy who didn't know "without".

now having to live with
whatever he's allowed.

fully realizing his life
was complete,
since it's too late.

his last chance candle
has burnt out at both ends.

now he's just free-falling
through life like a sky-diver
without a parachute.

expecting the same violent impact,
...any second now.

Extremities

Jeremy Cisneros

They told me but I would *not* listen. They had no right to tell *me. I knew better.* The weather would not get worse because there was no storm coming.

The day was sunny and bright. The snow glistened and sparkled like shards of glass from the reflected rays. Over the soft mountains tops I saw the growing darkness eat up the light. I realized I was wrong about the storm. The calm would not last long.

Descending down the mountain while listening to the crunch of the snow beneath my snowshoes felt strangely peaceful. The outing was supposed to last all day but it was still early and I had to call it quits. After a few moments I noticed that the brightness, completely faded, was replaced by a blanket of cold and dark. The wind peaked and snow began to swirl around me. Before I knew it, those flakes of snow became a full-on blizzard.

Panic started creeping into my mind and I had begun to regret being so reckless. Forcing one snowshoe in front of the other as fast as possible was a mistake. Balance escaped me and I began to tumble. End over end, down the mountain I went. I thought it would go on forever until my body suddenly stopped. The pain in my leg took my breath away, however it was the audible crack I had heard and felt in my chest that scared me the most. Full panic moved into my mind and consumed me. *It paralyzed me*.

The snow and wind were too violent to be able to see ahead at all. I attempted to stand but trying quickly brought me to my knees and I realized it would not be possible. I knew of a cabin around here somewhere on this side of the mountain. It had to be close but I had no idea where. Maybe it was Providence looking out for me that after a moment of trying to gather my thoughts, I had realized it was this very cabin that stopped my tumble. The roof, covered thickly in feet of snow loomed in front of me through the oppressive sky, howling wind, and swirling snow. This cabin was now my island, my savior. I managed to crawl around it until I finally spotted what looked like a way inside. The top of a crude door was exposed enough to be my way in. Lying on my side and giving a few hard, bone-jarring kicks, I had loosened up the door enough to throw my small pack into the cabin. My hands numbed as I scooped enough snow away from the door to slip headfirst into the musty, dark void. The pain in my leg was overwhelming. I closed the door and leaned against it while sitting on the floor. Darkness welcomed me like an old friend as I sought relief from the wind and the cold, Exhaustion claimed me through the mind-numbing pain in my leg and I allowed it to cradle me into a deep and dreamless sleep.

I awoke some time later to find the same pitch black that knew me before I slept. The storm was in full force outside and in fact seemed worse. One of the first things I noticed was the numb throbbing in my lower leg. Reaching down to where the pain was I understood, even in this ocean of dark, that below my knee a piece of bone ripped my skin and was no longer inside my leg. I removed the scarf from around my neck and quickly tied it around the break as tight as I could possibly bear.

My vision went white and pain seared as I tied the knot.

I began to crawl around within the cabin to find my bearings. I used my hands to see the way a blind man would do. Fumbling around, my hands saw and recognized a small stove. Locating the opening I placed a few twigs I had felt on the floor in the stove. Grabbing my pack, it was easy to find the small box of matches I knew were there. I remember hoping they were not wet. I selected one in the dark and struck it on my pant leg. It flared to life and light suddenly pushed away the darkness opening a new world.

Fire sustains. It felt so good on my cold body. I looked through the dim flicker of light down at my leg. It was busted up real good. The shiny tell-tale sign of blood was soaking the scarf I had tied around the break. Looking around, I noticed the cabin had been abandoned for some time. There was a small stack of about 15 logs by the stove, an old chair, a metal frame that was once a cot, and a shelf with seemingly random items. Everything lay silently asleep beneath a thick layer of dust.

No one had been in this cabin for a while, and it could have been used as a rest stop for miners who went west in ‘49. They were known for leaving meager supplies in places like this for others who were following them west. The problem was that this place was not on any trail. It was forgotten. There was a familiar feeling growing inside me and I slowly realized I was hungry. Knowing the storm raging outside would be over soon, I ate all of the small block of cheese and hard round of bread that were packed for my day of snowshoeing, and drank the rest of the water in my canteen. Listening to the storm from inside left a dreadful and ominous feeling in mind. *How long would it continue? How long would I be here?* It was inevitable that hunger and thirst would force their way into my body again. Finding an old skillet among the abandoned remains inside this cabin, I cracked the door open to scoop out some snow melt and was greeted by a vertical wall of snow. There was then no doubt in my mind that the snow completely covered the cabin. My hope evaporated with this revelation.

It became a sort of routine to carve snow from the wall with my small knife into the pot. I drank what was melted and washed my dressings. Even though I tried my best to be clean, I could smell the sourness of the infection. Water would be no problem but it was the lack of food that concerned me. I could only live several days without it.

Days crept by slowly or at least what I judged to be days. There was no way of knowing if it was day or night. The light could not penetrate the thickness of the snow, and the storm continued for what seemed like an eternity. Time seemed like it lacked a beginning or an end. Fear has totally consumed me. I was alone. I could die here.

I was angry and I was scared. I thought that my mind had been hallucinating in order to stimulate itself. Sweat soaked my body and there was a new pain: hunger. The pain gripped me, threw me down, and forced me to cry out. This was the most terrifying.

One day, or night, I found myself floating above me and remember thinking that it was weird. I saw a man lying there, resigned to a fate. He didn't look like anyone recognizable, yet somehow I knew it was me. I looked pathetic. Hunger had wrecked me and fear owned me. I was above myself when *he* got the idea. Watching me pull the knife out caused me to freeze. My mind was cloudy and I was confused. The small blade reflected light from the flicker of the stove. This was awful and painful to watch. Below, I placed a small stick into my mouth and lined up the blade where it was to cut. Effortlessly the blade drew out the blood. Slowly at first, then it coated the knife and pooled on the floor. It took some effort, and with some back and forth saw-like strokes, it was over. The pain brought me back and I was no longer above myself but returned to the floor. I looked down at what I had done and quickly wrapped my leg to stop the blood. My broken lower leg was no longer attached. My body was no longer whole. The pain controlled me and the relief of losing consciousness was sweet. When I awoke, I began to sob, but I had an idea.

I picked up my knife again and knew I could survive. I cut into my severed leg and sliced small pieces off of it to fill the skillet. I was powerless to the hunger as I ate ravenously, forcing me to chew and swallow myself to soothe the ache within my body. When the thought came into my mind that it was *my leg* that was being devoured, my stomach turned and I retched it all. That desperation to live, to simply survive, eventually outweighed the nature of my meal. I then ate meagerly and whenever my body craved it. I had found that small strips cooked slowly in my own fat were quite tasteless, but were at the same time the most flavorful. My body was then sustaining itself.

Eventually, the meat from my leg was gone. All that remained were my bones I used for a broth that I sipped and enjoyed hot. There was no way that consuming any additional parts of my body could be justified. *Unless?* No. Maybe, my *fingers? The toes of my lonely remaining foot? A slice of my leg, rear, or belly?* I was ashamed that I had considered it at all. Even wrestled with it. I would rather die than partake of my own body again.

It had been days, I think, and the need and desires to eat tortured me. There was no way of truly knowing when I last ate. The only way to judge was by the pains that controlled me, and they were terrible. They will win. I was so numb and past feeling that I did not even wince at the removal of my fingers one by one. Soon my hand would follow, all the way up to the wrist. I had eaten to fill my body but my soul was not satisfied. I was a shell of what used to be a man.

I now realize that there is no way I will be able to get out and make it to help. I resign myself to sit down. I stuff the last remaining logs into the fire and it will prove to be too much, just like I hope. The fire escapes and crawls up the walls of the cabin. The interior of my tomb brightens and the heat it glorious. I begin to laugh. My chin drops to my chest and I weep. Relief has come and I am no longer hungry.

No one will find me until the next spring when a son and a father are curious about a small half-burnt cabin among a thicket of trees. My grave will not burn all the way down. The snow around will melt and put my fire out. The son will look at my charred remains and then to his father. With innocent eyes and a youthful curiosity, he will ask his father, "Pa, what happened here?"

Hoarder

Nathan Ybanez

I build the Tower of Babel
in my cell. I know
it didn't work last time.
God sent us sprawling
like a bad game of Jenga.
But I'm not trying
to reach heaven -
just hold back hell.

I collect newspaper,
coupons, scraps of
old letters, scrawled
midnight musings
heavily edited versions
of this poem - anything
that promises meaning
I arrange at the borders
of my desolation.

This maché feng shui
is an art of things
left undone:
frayed phrases, hanging
metaphors, half-
baked sentences.
Columns of 8 ½ x 11 bricks
that moan and coo and whisper
to clothe the terrible silence.

Clarity is overrated.

Each of my bricks
speaks its own tongue,
a cacophony rising
like mist, cloud or
a plenitude of veils
over a woman -
whatever preserves mystery.

One tower, erected
near my feet, watches
over me in my sleep.
Three stand beneath
my desk, a chain
not easily broken.
Other crawl organically
protecting me in ways
that defy explanation.
You can't plan too much.
You have to remember
to forget what
you've been ignoring.

Cells are like words.
They mean only
what we choose
to fill them with.
I fill mine
with everything.

In Wild Places

Rick Anderson

A scattering of ancient oak,
trunks twisted and tortured,
hold vigil over the skyline
of a pristine alpine escarpment.
Ice clings to its granite walls
upon whose rocky outcrops
raptors make their airy homes.
A solitary pine protruding
angles sharply towards the sky,
a silent, watchful outlier
above an expanse of aspen
swaying as one in the wind.

Effortlessly rising on warm thermals,
an eagle soars high overhead,
scanning his vast aerial dominion.
Down below, the dark timber
shields the forest denizen
from the element's hard hand.
Here, the tanager, the fox,
the deer and the lynx thrive
in harmonious coexistence
as the ever-observant owl
bears witness to this wilderness,
archivist to its mysteries.

Far from the imprint of man
life continues symbiotically
as it was always meant to.
There are no laws here

for those courageous,
no asylum for the meek,
no churches for the weak.
There are no boundaries
nor any instructions.
Freedom is a real thing.
It is here, only here,
in these wild places.

Insignificance

Rick Anderson

He sees it now,
the very moment of it,
when all the strings
inside him came apart:
that moment when he
began to change into
what he has become,
a caricature of integrity,
weak, detestable,
vilified.

It began with that smile.
Soon shared impulses
rekindled lost passions.
Subtle intimations led
to murmured invitations
then unrestrained rendezvous
grew into all those many secrets.
Indiscretion was inevitable.

When it all imploded,
as it always had to,
he found himself alone
in a cold emptiness,
a liminal existence
where each thought,
every inclination,
even memories
- especially memories -
Became irrelevant.

Secreted now
in a far-off keep
of hard stone and steel,
suppressed by the crush
of countless killing minutes,
he has come, at last,
to understand his place
in this vindictive world.
He is less than zero.
He is insignificant.

Yet a curiosity lingers.
His mind can't unsee
the million little things
he might have done
to find his way into
a different tomorrow.
While such thoughts may be
austere, morbid even,
isn't that human nature?
As meaningless as
a thing may become
everyone
will always be interested
in the aftermath.

I'm Alone

Christopher Ashley

God sent???
Help me understand
Why I'm meant?
Very little time was spent,
So much love was given
But unto me it was lent!
It laughed at me and left me, saying:
"You're such a beginner!"
In this life, love is not really love,
It's duplicated;
Recreated, human incinerated;
Selfishly regenerated.
Boy, life's so complicated…
No more invitations,
My door's left open all the time,
Guess everyone's on vacation.
And it's on my mind,
That comforts me
Through these times.
Yes, I need you; all my family
And strangers who may become friends
No matter the measure,
Big or small...I'm alone…

Strive

Secundino Martinez

How can we be a part of a system if
they're always trying to hold us down?
The more we want to stay afloat,
the more they want to make us drown.
Just the thought alone makes me want to shed a tear.
I will not live in fear.
I'm a warrior.
I am here, and damn it, you are too.
There's one thing left for me to do,
this is your cue,
STAY TRUE!
So many factors, so many things,
so many times, so many places
so many people with shady faces.
We have to find our inner peace
because passion we can't fake this.
We have to keep on trudging on what's right;
we can't forsake it.
There's so many things worth living for.
There's so many things worth dying for.
So much good and bad. I can't ignore, one thing for sure.
We have to tear it apart, build it back up,
and make improvements.
More money for students.
More freedom for families and
our government stops being stupid.
You're causing more tragedies
we need improvements not casualties.
Get our troops out of war.
I'm mad at the higher-ups who want money,

power and more.
They will ignore if we don't settle the score.
For what's right, we have to strive for,
we have to strive for!
Because nobody else will, and I'm not saying to kill.
I know we feel the same.
Life has a lot of pain.
We all have a brain.
There's balance between wild and tame.
Justice, the best type of fame.
Here's one thing I claim.
Do the right thing, but that saying has so much grey.
It's not just black and white.
There's so much in between.
Stand up tall, show compassion, don't be so mean.
We're all on this earth together,
we need peace and harmony.
I don't know if we'll ever achieve,
but I know we have to aim for a better future
because life is getting so crazy.
Put our work in, we can't be lazy.
If we want to improve, make a move on the daily.
Please, think of the children, think of the babies
we need patience to help our future generations
our future generations.

I Love This Jam

Secundino Martinez

If you were a melody,
you'd be stuck in my head all day long
singing you on repeat
I would post you on the Internet
as the greatest song ever
telling my family and friends
to check you out as a good tune,
without sounding creepy.
I would print your lyrics
and share them with everyone possible
from downtown to down-under
the words of you would be memorized.
You would be carved into desks
of every schoolboy and college guy.
Graffiti Artists would spray paint
you on billboards, trains, subways
and sides of buildings,
bridges and underpasses.
All would see your name
people could read your message.
Speaking of Billboards,
the greatest singer in the world
would sing you,
making you the anthem of the universe
topping the charts all the way
through the heavens…
If you were a melody
I would say
"I Love This Jam."

Odd

Michael Severson

Startling silences.
Unfettered laughs.

Can’t get comfortable
feeling like I don’t belong
in my own skin.

Wanting the darkness to reign.

Fumbling fingers flickering through life,
forever finding folly.

Cold sweats, fevered trembles
when expected to commit,
Can’t, won’t, shouldn’t
make decisions.

You ask too much.
I expect too much.

Chewed lips, gnawed nails
sour stomach, bald pates.
Infinite problems to solve.
Never enough courage.

Smog is clogging up my already
fogged up brain,
slowing already retarded thoughts.

Heart on autopilot
the only part of me
that can enjoy its choices.

My conscience hating it every day.
Wanting to have that much strength.
Never pleading for assistance.

Chaos abounds in synaptic bursts
my innocence missing,
never sure of its existence.
Life on the outside
just as muddled.

Promises broken wide open
to show my masses my
pain and crushed hope.

Quiet sobbing behind my
cracked smiling mask and
never getting that release of
pressure that tears are
expected to give.

The apex that my life
has finally reached is still
below the surface of
everyday.

The Answer

Michael Severson

Silence is what I got
when I asked why.

Silence is what was left
when I said I don't cry.

Silence is the uncomfortable
beast in the room
when the judgement was
a heavy sigh.

Silence was the sad emotion
when I said goodbye.

Silence was the sound I made
when they said just try.

Silence was the feeling
when I said we'll get by.

Silence was the shout
when I said Hi.

Silence was the look
when I touched her thigh.

Silence was the answer
when I relayed my alibi.

Silence is something

I can't abide.

Silence is what we need
when they say die.

Of Memory and Form

Nathan Ybanez

Heaven is a puzzle fit together,
A mosaic of whispers
Between the minutes and hours.

It is dawn, with a soft breath,
Murmurs of dreams rising
Like mist from lips,
Kissing softly till eyelids flutter
And we sing butterfly good mornings.

It is rich crunch of toast,
Whistle-blow over anemic coffee
Just the way you like it
Always the way you like it:
Eggs and jam and sneaky peeks
At bare legs in sunshine -
And laughter. *Always* laughter,
At nothing. And everything.

It is arms curled around me
Suddenly, like a backpack,
Weight pressed into me
While I'm concentrating
On the wrong thing
That is the right thing
The only thing -
Perfume and rumpled fabric,
Calloused hands on peach-fuzz skin
Tightening at my touch
Brushing me away mischievously

Saying, "*Get back to work!*"

It is work in the garden,
Scrape of trowel clump of
Heady earth springy green
Dance of leaf and stem
As you cradle them
With gloved hands -
Your hair pulled back,
I ask you to explain
Something I already know
Just so I can hear you talk
Hear you say I can
Get my hands dirty.

It is black nails tracing
Black bruises, gently, slowly
Purple spreading over skin
Across sky, sun going down,
Golden sun, honeyed sun.
Your irritated voice exclaiming
Be more careful, Doesn't it hurt?
But all I can feel is you.

It is night, warm glow
Of flickering television
Whispers of the moon
Cascading through chimes,
Hand on mine
On the balcony
Palm squeezing
Saying everything
Not saying anything,

Bearing witness
To the copper-roofed hillside
Distant groan of ocean
The confluence of things,
The confluence.

Heaven is the sigh
As you lie beside me
Moist breath on neck,
Adjusting, arm draped over
Scrunching to my shape,
Closing your eyes
Feeling it's safe to slip
Into the black pool of sleep,
To let your edges bleed,
To release while holding tight
Knowing I will capture every drop
And call you back to me
When the mist is rising
And whispering of memory and form.

Postcard Confessions

Rick Anderson

I don't mind that you're staring.
I know my scars frighten.
Looking in mirrors used to scare me too
but I don't mind anymore.
Not anymore.

It's alright to look,
they can't hurt you.
Glance over these momentos,
these strange trophies,
marking those times, places and people
that made me stand stronger,
that took me to the ground.

I wonder what you see.
Does this jagged slash across my jaw line
remind you of the markings
found on a treasure map?
Is the wreckage on my neck
a mysterious hieroglyph?
Are the webworks of my eyes
the ingenious graffiti of an artisanal hand?
Your imaginings could be true…

Yet if I'm to be honest
they're just crumpled postcards
faded by the passing of time
And blemished by rough handling
or grainy, oft-visited snapshots
collected over the years

traveling dusty washboard backroads,
within bustling concrete mazes
and riding rickety, old barstools.
I hear their silent cautionary tales
of impulse and reaction,
of skirmish and liaison,
along the zigzagging byways
of impetuous existence.

They come back to me still
in the everyday reflections of glass and mirrors
through most often in judgmental eyes.
Each bears a single common message:
'Return to Sender'
Nobody wants them.
They've already enough of their own.
You can look, if you want, though.
I hope you will...want to.

Silence in Everything

Matthew LaBonte

I have become accustomed to silence.
it was not always the case
I have spent lifetimes
chasing the ever-alluring echo
rebounding from the arms of absence

In madness born of innocent furor
I raced with childish joy
through towering trees of giant girth
whose branches creak and moan
The swaying dirge of ancient grove
and seedling's search for growth
under stoic sentinel peaks above
whose crag-bodied careless shrugs
send rumbling showers of stone and slate
thundering down their slopes

across far-flung storm lashed prairie wide
electric air charged with rainwashed windsong
blond stalks rustling carapace whisper
as ground drinks greedily from sky bounty

cricket chirp and bullfrog roar
distant splash of leaping fish
fire crackle, jackal laughter
unseen hunter's cry

forest chorus city chatter
hungry for it all

to see, to hear
to feel, to taste
to touch, to be
but there is more…

For in the maelstrom
amidst the tumult and the glee
in leaf between and under stone
through lightning readied pause

between every creature's bated breath
and the distance to the stars
there is hush, a simple little thing

an emptiness so full
it seems a living thing
this, my friend, is silence
the space without which, echo cannot sing.

The Ghosts Are Laughing

Rick Anderson

Within the bony armor
of this disordered mind
ticks a callous timepiece;
a ruthless agent of judgement
there to punish, to remind.
Like slowly dripping water
its monotony is unrelenting,
straining the thin threads
suspending my desperation.
Its claw-like hands reach out,
slashing honed razors,
each tick slicing deeply
into my tenuous sanity.
Teetering over the edge
I topple into affectless isolation
and the refuge of memory.

I try but can't remember
that one last moment
of contented silence,
that perfect frame of
simple, sweet stillness.
And I can't always discern
realities from fantasies,
or truths from imaginings,
inside my mental carnival.
Confused and perplexed,
I ask the questions aloud
but the ghosts only laugh.

They already know the things
I have yet to learn
in the hardest of ways.

Inevitably I will learn
- I am learning -
that being alone,
being lonely always,
being nothing forevermore
is a burden far greater
than I have ever known
and I cannot bear it.
So, like the ghosts before me
I will dream of The Boatman
and passage into the void
to surrender myself
unto the Timekeeper
and beg him to stop the clock.

This Too Shall Pass

Christopher Shetskie-McAllister

The sweetest flavor
I can remember
from a life I lived before

was knowing I existed
in my most beautiful form
held in the warmest place
of a loving mind
that I adored.

Like,
the memory of a dream

dissolving...

Like cotton candy
left out
in the rain.

resurrection zen

(a poem for poets in 24/7 lockdown)

Wayne A. Gilbert

everything is reflected in the mirror at the pivot of nothingness
~Roshi Danin Katagiri

I know a man raised himself
a Dickensian orphan buried alive
concrete vault inside concrete
vault wrapped in razor wire
circled by a 4000 - volt kill fence

I know a man raised himself
inside his own body which he
fortified with blocks or marble
he quarried from the violent noise
piped into his sarcophagus
by old testament judges
who preside over the city tombs

I know a man raised himself
all the way to sitting cross-legged
a voiceless beardless sadhu
bent broken conjurer if
butterfly clouds a jazzy quarter
of larks right out of Shelley

I know a man raised himself
with no god there to push the weight
no trickster deity to shout “April fool”

only the empty universe before it banged
to teach him how to live among corpses
bunkered side by side without names

I know a man raised himself
discovered blood blackens as it dries
like ink he could use with a contraband
needle to compose tattoo poems
drive wounds deep into his living flesh
far enough to touch sands in Cape Town

I know a man raised himself
to listen for the lamentations
poured over crossed rebar
chalky bone-meal marker slabs
craned one-by-one side-by-side
"correctional" barriers for the dead

I know a man raised himself
an insurgency of soft-soled high-tops
for sun-dancing in high plains lockdowns
hitching rides on gull caws
above the ancient Colorado sea-bottom

I know a man raised himself
to stand tall among somnambulates
chant to himself "the chant of dilation and pride"
trying not to shine so brightly
the sniper will find him in the crosshairs

I know this main raised himself
in maximum oblivion
forced to be a monk though

called to be a lover
I've seen him
take long walks in high country meadows
zen gardens cathedral labyrinths
along the beach
without opening his eyes

I know this man raised himself
will find his way

January 2018

The Lyrical Vagabonds

Rick Anderson 157264
Rick typed these words onto the computer which was necessary for the completion of this book. He made himself available to every writer in the program regardless of their skill level. He is the Most Valuable Player in this entire production and the charging influence for the book. ~Editor

Christopher Ashley 102549
Imagine always being lost but trying your hardest to be found. Well, that's me; like in Castaway, drifting at sea…Love.

Felicion Charles 165910
Mr. Charles is "Black Superman," and he leaps metaphors in a single bound! There is no euphemism that he can't handle, no critique or writer's block that can keep him down. He is invincible! ~Editor

Jeremy Cisneros
…is an enigmatic yet simple guy; a lover of all things Colorado as well as his supportive family—is grateful of life and the blessings from heaven especially the ones not deserved! He is learning how to live life and recover from being a life-long selfish idiot, as well as trying to be contrite and astute.

Matthew LaBonte
Loves cake, yearns for coffee, and will eventually became a caricature of himself. Carpe Diem.

Secundino Martinez 168188
AKA "Dino." Born in Denver, Colorado in January of 1993. Raised in Longmont, Colorado. I'm currently serving a Life Sentence but I plan to get out and return to my amazing family.

Vern Mitchell 62245
Thank You, Swimming with Elephants Publishing, and Thank You Wyandotte County, Kansas. Go Chiefs, Super Bowl Champions!

Michael Severson 126144
Was born and raised in the wonderful State of Colorado, which he loves completely. He lives by the saying, "It's better to have it and not need it than to need it and not have it!"

Christopher Shetskie-McAllister 92178
I am, a memory in progress. An immovable traveler painting scenic vistas from every faraway world that visits me; simple in my complexity; locked away, yet still believing that I'm free to re-write my future; beyond tragedy and hope.

Manuel G. Sisneros, Sr. 97704
A proud Husband, Father and Grandfather. I have found that writing poems is comforting to my soul. For it took a place of solitude for me to realize that with my thoughts I was never alone, and when you place the sky as your roof you are bound by no limits.

Grant Stewart 141159
He is a good young writer and poetry enthusiast. ~Editor

Emilliano Urioste 172741
...is how the state defines me. Freedom is how I define my life, it is the name I go by. It is what is called out by those who know me and seek the same sense within. In loving memory of my Grandmother Clara Abeita who gave me the name Damacio.

Timothy Wakefield 168204
He is a gifted writer and his sense of humor is infectious. He also loves playing Blues Harp Harmonicas. ~Editor

Nathan Ybanez
Professor Wayne Gilbert is loved by many, not only because he is a great poet, but because he is a great man. The medicine of poetry comes from its feeling, and Wayne showed us how to courageously feel what usually lies hidden. I will always be grateful.

Douglas L. Micco 124585 Author and Editor
I dedicate my writings to my Mom and Dad, and family who've never given up on me through my entire incarceration. For my friends who stood by me and defended me without judgement, gave me their love. I wish to thank the Colorado DOC for giving me the educational opportunities to go to college and graduate. For the Parole Programs and Pre-Release Classes, and for all of my Instructors who gave me their time and efforts to teach me. For the Deaf-Help groups and the many Outside Volunteers who drive hundreds of miles both ways for no pay but to ensure that our programs are set-up and on-time. This book is dedicated to our wonderful library and our awesome Library Staff who are every part of this book. For my Prairie Band

Potawatomi and Muscogee Creek Tribes. For my ancestors and those who came before me. For my United States Military Service Women and Men, our Veterans and those who paid the ultimate supreme sacrifice in the name of freedom. For my LGBTQ Community who face discrimination and prejudice yet answer with compassion, awareness and love. For my hometown of Lawrence, Kansas, which I miss dearly. For my fellow inmates both federal and state whom are some of the most talented and intelligent people I have ever met. Now go home and write your own story!

About the Editor

Douglas L. Micco 124585

He is American Indian who belongs to both the Prairie Band Potawatomi and Muscogee Creek Tribes. He is originally from Lawrence, Kansas and is currently assigned to the Sterling Correctional Facility in Sterling, Colorado. He is involved in Education, Art, Music, Athletics, and Library Programs.

"Strive not only to succeed, but to shine as well."

www.ingramcontent.com/pod-product-compliance
Lightning Source LLC
LaVergne TN
LVHW051009080826
845145LV00009B/2542

* 9 7 8 1 9 5 0 3 7 5 3 8 7 *